The Life of
Jack Prel...

by Lisa Benjamin
illustrated by Mary Teichman

HOUGHTON MIFFLIN HARCOURT
School Publishers

PHOTOGRAPHY CREDITS: **Cover**, **1,2,3** Courtesy of Jack Prelutsky. **4** James Kirkikis. **5** Courtesy of Jack Prelutsky. **7** Courtesy of Jack Prelutsky. **8** © UpperCut Images/SuperStock. **10** Artville. **11** Getty Images. **12** © Patrik Giardino/Corbis. **13**, **14** Courtesy of Jack Prelutsky.

Printed in China

ISBN-13: 978-0-547-02306-9
ISBN-10: 0-547-02306-5

12 13 14 15 0940 18 17 16 15 14
4500496268

Do you like poems? Do you like to laugh?

Jack Prelutsky is a poet. He writes poems that make people laugh. He writes about taco-flavored ice cream. He writes about having your nose between your toes or in your hair.

He has written more than 40 books of poetry. One book is called *It's Raining Pigs & Noodles*. Another is called *Something Big Has Been Here*.

This book is about Jack Prelutsky's life. This kind of book is called a biography.

Jack was born in 1940. He lived in New York City. Jack liked a lot of things when he was growing up. He liked music and drawing. But he did not like poetry because he thought poetry was boring. It did not make him laugh.

Jack loved singing, and he sang as often as he could. He went to the High School of Music and Art. There, teachers taught him music and art.

Jack always hoped to become a singer. He never dreamed he would become a poet.

When Jack grew up, he had many jobs. He was a taxi driver and also a furniture mover. He worked as an illustrator, too. An illustrator is someone who draws pictures.

Jack enjoyed working, but none of his jobs was quite what he wanted. He was looking for a job that would be exactly right for him.

Jack started to enjoy poetry. He learned that poems did not have to be serious.

Jack also learned that poetry could express his ideas. He could write about wishes or dreams. In fact, he could write about anything at all! In a poem, he could imagine that animals talk or pretend that trees can sing. He could even make people laugh!

Jack began to write poems. His friends read his poetry, and they laughed a lot.

One friend had a great idea. He wondered if Jack could sell his poetry, and he told Jack to show his poems to other people.

A WOLF IS AT THE LAUNDROMAT

A wolf is at the Laundromat,
it's not a wary stare-wolf,
it's short and fat, it tips its hat,
unlike a scary glare-wolf.

It combs its hair, it clips its toes,
it is a fairly rare wolf,
that's only there to clean its clothes —
it is a wash-and-wear-wolf.

[signature]

THIS POEM is from
THE NEW KID ON THE BLOCK

Jack took his poetry to a company where books are made. The company liked Jack's poems and they offered to make them into a book. Jack accepted their offer.

Jack's first book came out in 1967. It was called *A Gopher in the Garden and Other Animal Poems*. The poems were very silly. Many children read them, and they laughed a lot, too.

Jack was now a poet!

Over the years, Jack wrote many books full of funny poems. One poem is about a giant pizza, and another is about singing dragons!

One poem is about hotdogs that can fly. It is called "We're Fearless Flying Hotdogs." The hotdogs sail through the sky on fluttering wings.

Some of Jack's poems are about big, grand ideas. Other poems are about small, simple things like ice cream or noses.

Jack finds ideas for poems everywhere. He likes to eat spaghetti, so he wrote a poem about eating spaghetti!

Not all of Jack's poems are silly. Some are scary. One of his books is called *Nightmares: Poems to Trouble Your Sleep*. It is about mean monsters and dangerous dinosaurs.

Some people like Jack's silly poems, and some people like his scary poems. Some people like both kinds of poems.

Jack's poetry may be silly or it may be scary, but it is never boring. Children like reading his books. Grown-ups like them, too. Sometimes parents and children read his books together.

Jack has won many awards for his poetry. In 2006, he won an important prize. This prize honored him for being a great children's poet.

Jack Prelutsky lives in Seattle, Washington, with his wife Carolynn. He hopes children will always enjoy his poems and he hopes that they might want to become poets, too.

Jack hopes they will see,
How much fun poetry can be!

Responding

✓ **TARGET SKILL** **Understanding Characters** Copy the chart. In the first column, write things Jack Prelutsky liked as a boy. In the second column, write jobs he has had. In the third column, write what his poems are about.

As a boy	Jobs	Poems About
music drawing	taxi driver ?	spaghetti ?

Write About It

Text to World Sometimes Jack Prelutsky writes about dinosaurs. Write a few descriptive sentences about dinosaurs. Include details that you know about them.

accepted	pretend
express	prize
fluttering	taught
grand	wonder

✔ **TARGET SKILL** **Understanding Characters** Tell more about characters.

✔ **TARGET STRATEGY** **Analyze/Evaluate** Tell how you feel about the text, and why.

GENRE A **biography** tells about events in a person's life.